JBIOG
Pavlo
Allman, Barbara

Dance of the Swan : a story about
Anna Pavlova

Dance of the Swan

Dance of the Swan

A Story about Anna Pavlova

by Barbara Allman
illustrated by Shelly O. Haas

A Creative Minds Biography

Carolrhoda Books, Inc./Minneapolis

For John, my partner in the dance, and Shelby,
whose dance has just begun—B. A.

For Sharon, India's poetress in motion—S. O. H.

Text copyright © 2001 by Barbara Allman
Illustrations copyright © 2001 by Shelly O. Haas

Carolrhoda Books, Inc.
A division of Lerner Publishing Group
241 First Avenue North
Minneapolis, MN 55401 U.S.A.

Website address: www.lernerbooks.com

Library of Congress Cataloging-in-Publication Data

Allman, Barbara.
   Dance of the swan : a story about Anna Pavlova / by Barbara Allman;
illustrations by Shelly O. Haas.
       p.   cm. — (A creative minds biography)
   Includes bibliographical references (p.   ) and index.
   ISBN 1-57505-463-9
   1. Pavlova, Anna, 1881–1931—Juvenile literature. 2. Ballerinas—Russia
(Federation)—Biography—Juvenile literature. [1. Pavlova, Anna,
1881–1931. 2. Ballet dancers. 3. Women—Biography.] I. Haas, Shelly O.,
ill. II. Title. III. Series.
GV1785.P3 A817   2001
792.8'028'092—dc21   00-009614

Manufactured in the United States of America
1 2 3 4 5 6 – MA – 06 05 04 03 02 01

Table of Contents

1

The Ballet School

It seemed to Anna that she was about to enter a fairyland. The sleigh quietly slipped through the snowy, moonlit streets of St. Petersburg, Russia. Mother was giving eight-year-old Anna a special Christmas treat—her first trip to the Maryinsky Theatre to see the ballet. Many times, Mother had told Anna the fairy tale of *The Sleeping Beauty,* and tonight they would see the story come to life with dancing and music.

Anna trembled as the orchestra played the first strains of Tchaikovsky's music. When the curtain rose, she gave a cry of delight at what she saw. On stage stood a golden palace.

Anna watched as the familiar story unfolded. She opened her eyes wide as the wicked fairy arrived in a coach pulled by rats. She stared when the Lilac Fairy waved her magic wand to break the evil spell. How sad when Princess Aurora pricked her finger on a spindle and fell asleep for a hundred years. What joy when the handsome prince kissed Aurora to wake her! Anna was taken by the beautiful movements of the dancers as they told the story that she loved so well. That night at the theater, Anna discovered dance. It cast a spell of beauty that would shape her life.

Riding home in the sleigh, Anna asked her mother if she could learn to dance. Mother thought Anna wanted to learn ballroom dancing, and she said of course. But she did not understand what was in her little girl's heart. Anna wanted to dance the role of Princess Aurora in the ballet. That night, snug in her bed, Anna dreamed she was a ballerina who danced like a butterfly to beautiful music all her life.

Anna was born two months early on January 31, 1881, and she had been small and delicate ever since. Anna's mother, Liubov Pavlova, was a poor laundry-woman. Her husband had died when Anna was only two. He had been the only father Anna had known, but her real father was probably a successful Jewish banker. Anna and her mother depended upon each other and were very close.

For days after their trip to the theater, Anna begged her mother to take her to the Imperial Ballet School so she could learn to be a ballerina. Liubov explained to Anna that if she entered the Imperial Ballet School she would have to live there. She would only see her mother on holidays, weekends, and during the summers. Anna didn't want to leave her mother, but she had made up her mind to learn to dance. She wanted to be part of that beauty. When Mother said no, Anna's dark eyes pooled with tears.

Anna didn't give up pestering her mother, and Liubov kept thinking about Anna's wish to dance. The Russian government ran the ballet school, so education, room and board, and clothing were free for its students. In return, when the dancers graduated, they signed a contract to dance in the Russian Imperial Ballet. Anna's mother realized that her daughter would be well cared for and well educated. Finally, Mother gave in. She would take Anna to the ballet school.

As Anna and her mother arrived on Theatre Street, Anna peered up at the large school building with its lovely arched windows and second-story columns. The director of the school greeted Anna and her mother but had some disappointing news. The school would only accept children who were at least ten years old. Anna was told she would have to come back to apply in two years. So she and her mother went sadly home.

Anna's mother had taught her daughter to pray before the icon of the Virgin Mary in the living room of their small home. As Anna lit a candle, she made the sign of the cross. In her prayers, she told the Holy Mother of her dream of becoming a ballerina. She prayed the school would take her in.

On a warm summer day, when Anna was nine, she watched eagerly as chairs, tables, beds, dishes, and the giant *samovar* for making tea were packed into a wagon. As they did every summer, Anna and her mother were going to Ligovo to stay in their *dacha*— a cottage in the country.

Anna loved the little wooden cottage and the wild countryside around it. On the porch of the little cottage, Anna read aloud to her mother, and her mother taught her to sew. During the day, she studied the flowers closely, spoke to the birds, and danced with the butterflies. Best of all, she could imagine herself to be the Sleeping Beauty in the shady woods.

Summer days nourished Anna's soul, filling her with a love for nature's beauty.

When Anna turned ten, she reminded her mother that it was time to go back to the ballet school. Anna was tested in several school subjects and in physical grace and ability, and she also had a medical exam. Although she was smaller and frailer than some of the children, the examiners noticed Anna's natural grace. And so, in 1891, she was accepted into the Imperial Ballet School. On the day Anna left for school, she and her mother both cried. Though it was hard to leave, at last Anna's dreams were beginning to come true.

2

On Her Toes

When the eight o'clock bell rang, Anna awoke from her dreams. In the big dormitory room, twenty little girls jumped from their beds. They smoothed the striped bedcovers under the watchful eyes of their governess. Each morning, Anna dutifully took the spoonful of cod liver oil offered to her by the governess and swallowed it as quickly as she could. She disliked the awful-tasting stuff, but she didn't complain because she had been told a daily dose of it would make her strong.

Next Anna washed, put on the blue dress that was a schoolgirl's uniform, and joined the other girls in front of the icon for morning prayers. After prayers, she ate her breakfast of bread and butter and drank her tea. Then she was off to dance class.

Anna already felt at home in the big room, with its high ceilings, wood floors, and huge mirrors. While a musician played the violin, she and the other beginning dancers did exercises at the barre, a wooden rail attached to the wall. Anna lightly held on to the barre with one outstretched hand while doing her pliés—knee bends—with slow, graceful movements.

After lunch, Anna went for a walk with the other girls. More lessons followed until dinner at four o'clock. Then Anna was glad to have some free time with her classmates. Some evenings, she studied fencing, pantomime, acting, or music. But tonight she was rehearsing her part in a ballet to be given at the royal palace. Anna was dancing the role of a flower bud. In a few days, she and her classmates would dance for the Russian royal family.

After her long day, Anna was ready for supper at eight o'clock. She gladly slipped under the bedcovers at nine.

Anna's class often danced for the royal family. One day, after their performance, the children were having tea with the royal family. The king of Russia, Czar Alexander III, had noticed how well Anna's friend Stanislava danced her difficult steps. So the kindly czar paid Stanislava a compliment. As Anna watched the czar give her friend a hug and a kiss, tears of jealousy welled up in her eyes. She stamped her feet. She wanted a hug and kiss, too!

The czar's brother, Grand Duke Vladimir, laughed when he saw Anna stamp her feet. To make her feel better, the grand duke gave her a ride on his knee. But even that did not help. Anna was serious about her dancing, and she made up her mind that someday she would be noticed.

Anna was becoming accustomed to the well-ordered, disciplined world of the Russian Imperial Ballet. Her lessons were as well planned as everything else in the ballet system. The exercises she learned were carefully designed to strengthen her muscles. Only when she was strong enough was she allowed to begin training to dance on pointe—on the tips of her toes.

Near the end of ballet class, Anna excitedly slipped her feet into the toe shoes she had carefully darned. Then she tied the ribbons she had securely sewn on. At first, it was hard to stand on her toes, and she could only do it for a few seconds. How clumsy she felt!

With practice, Anna was able to walk on pointe. She watched as her teacher demonstrated some steps for the class. As the first small group of children repeated the steps, Anna watched them carefully. She listened as the teacher corrected the dancers. Anna found she could learn a good deal by always listening to the teacher's corrections, even if they weren't meant for her. When it was her group's turn, Anna stepped out into the center of the floor and placed her feet in position. She tried to remember each step and where to place her head, arms, and feet. There was so much to think about, all at one time.

Though Anna was a talented and hardworking student, her teacher thought she was too frail to become much of a dancer. Anna knew it was true that she had a smaller frame and was slimmer than most of the girls. Her delicate body type was not popular for dancers of her day. Dancers were supposed to look solid and sturdy, even plump. Still, Anna was steadfast in her desire to be a ballerina.

Another teacher told her class about a very great dancer of the past, Marie Taglioni. Taglioni had danced throughout Europe and made a great sensation when she came to St. Petersburg. She was thin and gently graceful, but very strong, and she was one of the first dancers to dance on her tiptoes. This made her appear lighter than air to her audiences. Anna heard about Taglioni's most famous role. In *La Sylphide,* a Romantic ballet in which she wore a flowing tutu, Taglioni danced the part of a beautiful, unearthly winged creature.

Marie Taglioni brought something new to dancing. She was more than just a strong technical dancer. She used her own creativity to give the dance a special beauty.

Anna knew that Marie Taglioni had become a great dancer even though she was petite and thin. This fueled Anna's hopes for her own future, and she dreamed of performing in foreign countries someday, as Taglioni had. Anna listened with great interest whenever her teacher spoke about the remarkable ballerina.

As Anna moved up through the ballet classes, her teachers paid attention to her unusual qualities. One of Anna's teachers, Pavel Gerdt, noticed Anna's natural grace. Gerdt told Anna to leave the acrobatic tricks to other dancers and allow her own special delicacy to shine. Her differences were something for her to build on, not to change. In Gerdt's classes, Anna learned how to give her lovely arms a softness and how to make a beautiful line with her arms and legs. He encouraged the girl with the dark, expressive eyes to be expressive in all her movements.

Anna tried hard to have the "turnout" that every dancer worked to achieve. In a good turnout, a dancer's legs rotate or turn out from the hip sockets, helping the dancer create a solid base with her feet, toes out to the sides. But another teacher, Christian Johansson, decided not to call attention to her turnout and make her work at something she couldn't change. Instead, Johansson helped Anna use her delicate frame to create a look of lightness when she danced. He knew she was a special dancer who deserved encouragement.

The Imperial Ballet School didn't only teach students to dance. It surrounded them with beauty of all kinds. Anna listened to the finest music and read good books. She went to the theater to see the best plays and to museums to see masterpiece paintings. She ate fine meals and learned to balance work with play. Her artistic nature took in the beauty that was all around her every day.

By 1898, when Anna was seventeen, her graduation was only a year away. She was eager to begin her career. She wanted to reflect the beauty she was surrounded by into the world, through her dancing.

Marius Petipa, the old and respected master of the Imperial Ballet School, often looked in on the dance classes. He knew the strengths of the students, especially the outstanding ones. Petipa was also a choreographer—he created dances by planning the movements and teaching them to the dancers—and he was quite famous.

As he watched Anna, Petipa was reminded of *The Two Stars,* a dance he had created years before. This dance would be perfect for Anna. For a school performance, Anna and her classmate Stanislava Belinskaya danced the lead roles with another student, a boy of exceptional talent named Michel Fokine. Michel was a handsome dreamer who was often lost in thought, creating his own dances.

Later that year, on October 21, the aristocratic audience in the pale-blue decorated Maryinsky Theatre glittered in their satins, jewels, ribbons, and official medals. Anna was still a student, but she was dancing in her first public appearance at the Maryinsky, the theater where she had first seen ballet as a child. "Almah" in *Daughter of the Pharaoh* was a minor role, but it was still a solo. In the second act, as she was doing turns, Anna felt her slipper catch on the stage. She tripped and fell with her back to the audience. Anna picked herself up gracefully and curtseyed a dignified apology to the crowd. It was a gesture that won them over. Anna was relieved. She was beginning to discover that she had a way of bringing out something from within her that spoke to the audience. They responded to her with affection.

Finally, the evening of her graduation performance arrived, April 11, 1899. Anna knew that in addition to the audience of royal and wealthy ballet patrons, judges from the school would be observing. She gave a delightful performance in *The Imaginary Dryads,* a dance that her teacher Pavel Gerdt had chosen because it would show off Anna's soft, flowing style.

During the performance, judges determined where the young dancers would fit into the Imperial Ballet. The ballet system was set up almost like an army. Anna knew that dancers started in the lower ranks and worked their way up, earning an official title at each step. Young dancers fresh out of school began as members of the corps de ballet, performing onstage as a large group. More accomplished dancers, the coryphée, danced in smaller, featured groups of three to six. Next came second soloist, then first soloist. Among soloists, only a very few extraordinary dancers were honored with the official title of ballerina. Once a ballerina was given a starring role in a ballet, it belonged only to her and could not be given to another dancer unless she approved.

The following day, when the results of the judging were announced, Anna learned she would not be a member of the corps de ballet. Instead, she had been promoted to coryphée! Anna had been granted an unusual honor by the school, and she was determined to prove her worthiness.

Anna didn't know that a new admirer had been seated in the audience at the Maryinsky Theatre the night of her graduation performance. Victor Dandré was an important member of the city council. He was from a French family, a thirty-year-old bachelor, and a great fan of the ballet. Anna Pavlova caught his eye, and he decided she was his favorite dancer of the evening.

Victor arranged to meet Anna, and from then on his adoration of her grew. Anna enjoyed Victor's company and his appealing French style.

Although her formal student days were over, Anna knew that she needed to continue her studies in order to earn the title of ballerina. She wanted to be the best. After graduation, she studied with Yevgenia Sokolova, who had been an outstanding ballerina herself. Anna worked as hard as ever.

Madame Sokolova believed a ballerina must continue her performance even after the dance is over, as she takes her bows. She taught Anna how to bow with special grace. Anna understood that curtain calls were part of the performance, when the audience and performer showed their feelings toward one another. As she stepped out onto the professional stage, Anna polished her bows. It was almost as if she sensed the acclaim that was to come her way.

3

Changes in the Air

The dignified white-haired gentleman held his cane in one hand and watched Anna with a sharp eye. Enrico Cecchetti had been a ballet star many years ago in Italy and had come to Russia. He was a master teacher who knew how to help dancers bring out their own style. Anna was now taking private lessons with him. Though she was one of the soloists in the Imperial Ballet, she still strove to improve her dancing. She wanted to become prima ballerina.

During Anna's two-hour lessons, Cecchetti worked with her to strengthen her back and polish the way she used her hands. As Cecchetti whistled a tuneful accompaniment, Anna concentrated on dancing the steps in the way he had instructed her.

Anna's hard work paid off. In *The Seasons,* the revered ballet master Marius Petipa created a role especially for her—the role of Hoarfrost. In the opening scene, Hoarfrost, Ice, Hail, and Snow danced around Winter, played by a male dancer.

Later in 1900, Anna danced the leading role of Flora in *The Awakening of Flora*. At first, she was partnered with her teacher Pavel Gerdt, and later with her old schoolmate Michel Fokine. But the choreography was not suited to Anna's light style, and she didn't have much success.

Then, in 1902, Anna was given the opportunity to dance the important role of Nikiya, an oriental temple dancer, in *La Bayadère*. Dancing to the soulful strains of a violin, Anna balanced on one leg and extended the other behind her. She seemed to roll her upper body into a ball. Then slowly unfolding her spine and stretching up, she held the tension in her body until she reached the top—and released it. Anna combined dancing and acting into one in a magnificent performance, and the critics thought she danced with inspiration. People began to compare her to the great Marie Taglioni.

By 1903, Anna had become a first soloist in the Imperial Ballet. Marius Petipa decided to restage an old-fashioned Romantic ballet, *Giselle*. The lead role was perfect for Anna, though it was usually danced by a ballerina, not a soloist. Anna knew she was extremely fortunate to dance the role of Giselle, the charming peasant girl who, betrayed by her lover, goes mad, dies, and returns as a ghostly dancer.

Anna began to prepare for her role, but before she could perform it, Petipa was removed from his post at the Imperial Ballet. Petipa was loved and respected by the dancers, but the directors wanted a new choreographer. *Giselle* would go on as scheduled, however. Even though Petipa was no longer at the school, Anna went to him for his expert coaching. She wanted to give her role her own distinctive touch, and Petipa could help her.

On the night of April 30, 1903, Anna prepared herself backstage as she always did in order to calm the nervous feelings she had before a performance. Standing in the wings, she pressed the toe of first one, then the other shoe into the resin box. The resin would help keep her shoes from slipping onstage. She stretched her back by bending forward and touching her hands to the floor, then straightened up and adjusted her costume at the waist. She did a simple exercise of pointing one foot at a time to the front, side, and back. She made the sign of the cross and waited for her cue.

In *Giselle,* Anna displayed her already great powers of expression to their utmost. She did not simply act out the famous scene where Giselle goes mad—she danced it. She used pieces from the beginning of the ballet, but danced them in a jumbled, confused way.

It was as if she were hearing a far-off voice. She put so much meaning into the story that one critic proclaimed she danced with her soul. She gave her audience an experience to remember.

In many of the ballets that Anna was dancing, she was partnered with Michel Fokine. Michel was a dependable partner. When she whispered to him to give her a little push to help her around as she spun on the pointe of one foot, he knew just how to hold her so the audience never saw the push. Anna had to completely trust Michel to support her in turns, balances, and lifts, and to catch her properly when she leapt into his arms.

When Anna and Michel took a break from rehearsals, they often found themselves in serious discussions about reforms that Michel felt were needed in the ballet. At the turn of the century, Russian ballets often focused more on the dancers themselves than on the story they were dancing. Ballerinas had current-day hairstyles. They wore their own jewelry onstage, even if it wasn't the style of their costume. The jewels were often gifts from wealthy ballet patrons, and the ballerinas would smile at their patrons from the stage during performances. Michel felt that costumes should reflect the time and place of the story. He thought the ballerinas should always be in character onstage, not smiling to their friends. Also, most choreographers used gestures in their ballets to show what the characters were speaking to each other. Only audience members who understood the gestures knew what was being "said." Michel felt that the story should be danced continuously, without the hard-to-understand gestures. Anna began to see that Michel had some good ideas for change.

Other dancers were also thinking of new ways to dance. Isadora Duncan arrived in St. Petersburg in December 1904, and her visit caused a sensation. Isadora was an American dancer whose creations were loose and free. She wore flowing Greek-style tunics and danced in her bare feet. Anna, Michel, and many of their friends eagerly went to see Isadora dance. Though Isadora's style was quite unlike the well-ordered Russian ballet, Anna liked Isadora's modern dancing. She invited Isadora to dinner at her apartment, along with Victor Dandré and several of her friends from the ballet. They enjoyed an evening of lively conversation about art and dance.

Change was in the air. It was a time of great interest in political reform in Russia. Political organizers wanted to help poor, working-class people. Strikes stopped the trains from running, and riots broke out in many parts of the country.

The army of Czar Nicolas II fired into a crowd of workers demonstrating in the street. Though Anna respected the czar, she was appalled.

Just as workers around Russia were questioning authority, so were the dancers of the Imperial Ballet. They began to have meetings to discuss their dissatisfaction with the directors of the Imperial Ballet. Anna and Michel were among the leaders at these meetings. Above everything in life, art was supreme to Anna. On this principle, she spoke out for artistic freedom.

The dancers wanted more say in how things were run. They wanted Marius Petipa back. They wanted the school's curriculum to include classes in history of the arts, and they wanted changes in hours and pay. The dancers presented a petition with their demands and over two hundred signatures to the directors. The directors didn't respond, so the dancers went on strike, refusing to perform. The directors threatened that if the ballet closed the dancers would lose their jobs. They continued to put pressure on the dancers and posted a notice for the dancers to sign showing their loyalty.

One of the dancers, Sergei Legat, took his own life in distress over the situation. At his funeral, Anna made sure that a wreath of flowers was displayed for everyone to see. The ribbons on it were printed with the words "To the first victim at the dawn of the freedom of art from the newly united ballet company."

In the end, a committee was formed to make changes, but very few reforms were actually carried out. Anna was given a warning, but the directors did not want to lose her exceptional talents. And although Anna wanted more artistic freedom, she didn't want to endanger her career. Before long, the directors forgave her radical actions. Later that same year, 1905, Anna was promoted to prima ballerina.

4

The Swan

The sun unfolded its evening glow across the sky as Anna relaxed and enjoyed the view of the shoreline. Anna, Victor Dandré, and Michel Fokine were driving outside St. Petersburg. When Anna spotted a beautiful swan near the water's edge, she wanted to feed it. She remembered the leftover sandwiches she had and asked Victor to stop the car. Anna climbed out, unwrapped the sandwiches, and coaxed the swan with some morsels. Michel was taken by the scene of the graceful dancer in white reaching out to the delicate bird.

A few months later, Anna was invited to dance at a charity performance for the newborn babies of poor mothers, and she accepted. She asked Michel Fokine if he would choreograph a new solo for her. He had been practicing a mandolin version of *Carnival of the Animals* by Camille Saint-Saëns. Remembering the evening when Anna had fed the swan, he thought of one part of the music, "The Swan." It would make a good accompaniment for this dance.

Michel described how he pictured the dance of the swan to Anna. The dance would tell the story of a dying swan with a fiery and majestic spirit, making an unsuccessful effort to soar one last time. Then Michel demonstrated his ideas for Anna while she followed along behind him. Anna could almost feel what Michel had in mind before he did it—they had danced together so often. In about half an hour, the dance was complete. Anna loved the new dance for its use of expressive movements. And the subject of the dance—nature—was always close to Anna's heart.

The Dying Swan was premiered at the charity performance on December 22, 1907. Backstage at the Maryinsky, Anna went through the same ritual she always did to calm herself and to sink into the role she would dance.

Then, to the gentle melodies of a cello and harp, the swan entered from stage left. With her back to the audience, Anna seemed to skim across the stage as on a smooth, glassy pond. Her feet moved in small, swift pas de bourrée—crossed steps on pointe. Her soft arms and tiny fingers made rippling movements as they became the wings of the swan, reaching high and then dropping low. Her long, graceful neck supported her feather-rimmed head as it made tiny, quick, bird-like movements. She seemed to use every inch of her being to express the spirit of the struggling bird. Anna did not only dance the part, she *became* it. Finally, as the swan collapsed to the ground, an arm reached up, up—and delicately came down.

The audience sat breathless with emotion for a brief moment before bursting into enthusiastic applause. *The Dying Swan* was an instant success.

In the summer of 1908, Anna made her first foreign tour. With a group of dancers from the Imperial Ballet, she traveled throughout Scandinavia and to Prague and Berlin. Her audiences had never before seen Russian ballet, and both the critics and the public praised her artistry. In Stockholm, the king came to the theater every night. He invited Anna to the palace to tell her how much he had enjoyed her dancing, especially the Spanish dance she had performed.

One evening in Stockholm, a crowd of people followed her from the theater to her hotel. The crowd stood silently below her window until Anna stepped out onto the balcony. Then the crowd erupted with loud cheers and a serenade. Anna was deeply touched by this demonstration of affection. As a gesture of thanks, she tossed the flowers she had received onstage that evening into the crowd. Returning inside, Anna wondered aloud what she had done to deserve such adoration.

Her maid answered that she had given people an hour of beauty and happiness, helping them to forget for a while the sorrows of everyday life.

Anna began to realize that she was an ambassador for her art, just as Marie Taglioni had been. She was bringing the beauty of ballet to people who had never seen or appreciated classical dance before.

The next season, 1909, the great arts promoter Sergey Diaghilev invited Anna to perform in Paris with his Ballet Russe in its opening season. Diaghilev wanted to produce a Russian ballet season in Paris because he felt sure that it would be a sensation there. He was planning a season with the greatest Russian stars. Anna agreed to go to Paris that summer, but first she had other engagements to fulfill.

Anna danced at the Maryinsky Theatre and again went on tour with dancers from the Imperial Ballet. Audiences in Berlin and Vienna loved her, but the newspaper critics were harsh. In their view, Anna's thin figure was ugly. They thought she couldn't compare to the shapely German and Austrian dancers to whom they were accustomed. Anna tried to ignore their comments and focus on her dancing.

Anna's ballet shoes were very important to her. Before a performance, she went through pair after pair to find shoes that fit properly, and she rarely felt they were perfect. Anna's shoes were made especially for her in Milan, Italy, by a craftsman named Romeo Nicolini. He made them by hand to her specifications, and he tried his best to please her. Sometimes Anna sent him drawings and measurements. When she was in Italy, she went to see Nicolini to demonstrate some steps so he could see how the shoes needed to fit. The shoemaker was honored that Anna wore his shoes. Even so, he told her old teacher Enrico Cecchetti that he was glad he had only one Pavlova to please, or it would be the end of him.

All over Paris that summer, posters with Anna's likeness had been hung. Parisians were waiting to see the great Pavlova. When Anna arrived, the season had already begun.

Anna danced with the Ballet Russe for six performances. One of her partners was Vaslav Nijinsky, a brilliant dancer who had been a few years behind Anna in school. When Nijinsky danced, the Parisians marveled at his amazing leaps. He seemed to pause in midair before coming back to earth. As a pair, Anna and Vaslav were matchless.

Anna also danced with Michel Fokine in a dance called *Egyptian Nights*. Michel knew that Anna held Taglioni as her ideal, but he thought Anna had outdone even Marie Taglioni.

Anna was an instant success, making front-page news. Her artistry moved her audiences so much that one critic declared she had a sacred fire within her. She was invited to London to perform at a private party attended by the king and queen. Wearing a copy of one of Marie Taglioni's dresses, she danced with Mikhail Mordkin as her partner. Anna had danced with Mikhail a few years earlier in Moscow. He had a strong, masculine build that complemented Anna's delicate form onstage. Anna admired Mikhail's dancing and thought he was a good actor as well. Anna also danced an impromptu Spanish dance to one of the queen's favorite tunes. For the last dance, Anna wore a Russian folk costume. At the end of the dance, the Russian costume made it difficult for her to step down from the stage to greet the king. Anna was enchanted when the king himself stepped forward to help her down.

Before leaving England, Anna and Mikhail Mordkin signed contracts to return and perform at the Palace Theatre. First, however, Anna returned to St. Petersburg to dance at the Maryinsky, then she and Mikhail were off to New York.

When the steamship carrying the Imperial Ballet dancers docked in New York, Anna was relieved. She had been seasick for most of the trip, but she was eagerly looking forward to her debut at the Metropolitan Opera House.

On February 28, 1910, the night's program included a complete opera, so the ballet did not begin until after eleven o'clock. Around midnight, Anna made her entrance in the first act of *Coppélia.* The audience hadn't known what to expect of Russian ballet, but soon they became enchanted with Anna's dancing. When Anna and Mikhail took their last bow to thunderous applause, it was after one o'clock in the morning, and the theater was still packed.

The dancers from the Imperial Ballet performed in New York, Boston, and Baltimore before sailing back to Europe. Anna's first trip to America had been a huge success, and she knew she would return. She planned to create her own troupe of dancers.

Despite all of her triumphs, Anna felt herself tremble as she made her entrance onto the stage of the Palace Theatre in London on April 18, 1910. This was her first time dancing for the English public.

When the dance ended, Anna felt as if the world had stopped. There was complete silence—then shouts and applause. Laughing and crying at the same time, Anna reached out to her audience as she took her bows. The petite ballerina, the incomparable Pavlova, had won another victory for her art.

5

Ambassador of Dance

A strong bond of affection existed between Anna and Victor Dandré. Anna had come to depend on Victor in hundreds of ways, both large and small, and Victor adored Anna. His skill in business and in arranging tours allowed Anna to concentrate on her work. Anna kept their marriage secret from the press. She understood that dance is illusion—making the most difficult movements seem light and easy. To Anna, the dancer must present an illusion offstage as well—an image of romance and glamour. So she preferred to keep her private life private.

Anna spent less and less time in Russia. Victor had some business problems in Russia, and they both loved England and decided to live there. Anna and Victor found a house in the outskirts of London. Anna fell in love with Ivy House the first time she saw it. The house had a large, open room in the center. It was two stories high with a balcony all around it. This could be Anna's studio and rehearsal hall. There was a pond and more than an acre of lawn and garden. The pond would be a perfect home for swans

On a delightful, breezy June day in 1912, Anna hosted a garden party at her new home. Late in the afternoon, she appeared dressed as a shepherdess, with golden sandals and flowers in her hair. She and her new ballet partner, Laurent Novikoff, danced on the grass to entertain the guests.

Anna had long dreamed of teaching young dancers, and her new studio at Ivy House was ideal for giving lessons. At the age of thirty-one, she began teaching a small group of carefully chosen young girls. The girls worked hard to please Madame, as they called their teacher. She gave them four lessons a week. But all was not work. Sometimes the girls ran down to the pond to see Madame's pet swan, Jack. Jack would come only when Madame called him. Then he would curl his long neck around her in an embrace.

After months of lessons and weeks of Sunday rehearsals, the young girls were ready for their performance with Madame at the Palace Theatre. Anna, who always paid attention to the smallest detail, darned their toe shoes herself in the car on the way to the theater. She didn't want anyone to slip onstage.

For the dance, the girls were all dressed as flowers and Anna as a butterfly. They gave a charming performance, and Anna was pleased with her pupils.

Although Anna loved Ivy House, it seemed she never stayed there long. She wanted to share her art with as many people as possible, so she formed her own ballet company for touring. Victor arranged tours for her troupe and traveled with them.

Unlike the Imperial Ballet, where Anna was educated, her company was not funded by a government. It was not easy to maintain a troupe of traveling performers. But Anna Pavlova was in demand wherever she went. This meant that even with travel expenses, scenery, and costumes, the company could make money. Anna made sure Victor paid her dancers good wages.

Tours of North America took Anna's troupe across the continent, with eight to eleven performances a week. Most often, she gave one performance a night, each in a different city or town. Most ballerinas would not have even considered dancing that often— the schedule was too exhausting. Sometimes Anna's company would even give a matinee in one city and an evening performance in another. Wardrobe assistants and stagehands had to pack and load scenery and trunks of costumes, then unload them all again when they arrived in the next town.

When she arrived in a town, Anna would speak to the press and then go straight to the theater to practice. Anna knew that a dancer must work constantly to stay in shape for performing. She held her dancers to the same high standards of professionalism, but truthfully, no one worked harder than Anna.

Anna thrilled audiences wherever she went. Dance reviewers often commented on her amazing arabesques. An arabesque is a pose on one foot with the other leg extended in back. Anna could balance in an arabesque on the toes of one foot for a very long time, with complete stillness. She could do a set of turns and then stop motionless in an arabesque.

In *Amarilla,* Anna danced the role of a gypsy. Shaking her tambourine, she traveled backward smoothly and with lightning speed in arabesque. She made it all look easy and natural, when in fact it was extremely difficult.

Anna never performed such technical feats just to dazzle her audience—she used them to serve the story. She could dance the way she did because her feet had remarkably strong arches. But the way that she thought about her dancing allowed her to do even more. When Anna went up on pointe in an arabesque, she began by thinking first of the toes, then the ankle, the calf, the knee, and so on up to the top of her head.

When she got to the top, it was time to go on to the next movement. When Anna held an arabesque, the conductor would watch her carefully and direct the orchestra to hold the music until she was ready to move on.

Anna rarely allowed illness to keep her from dancing. She did not want to disappoint her audience. In Los Angeles, she had a sore throat and a high fever, but she insisted on performing in the afternoon matinee. The audience never suspected that every time she made an exit she collapsed backstage. When she became delirious, talking about a bouquet that wasn't there, a doctor insisted on taking her to the hospital. Anna went to the hospital, but she came back for the performance that evening. Then she boarded a train for San Francisco and her next performance.

Later in the tour, in St. Louis, she hurt her left ankle and had to be carried to her dressing room. After she recovered enough to dance, the ankle was still painful. Anna told reporters that her *right* ankle had been hurt. That way, she confided to her dancers, people would be looking at the wrong ankle when she danced, and everything would look fine.

In the summer of 1914, war broke out between Russia and Germany. Anna was returning from Russia through Germany, but she managed to get safely back to England. The terrible conflict that gripped Europe soon became known as the Great War.

Because of the war, Anna made plans to leave for another tour of the United States. By the autumn of 1914, she was performing with her company in such places as New York, Buffalo, Syracuse, Scranton, Philadelphia, Richmond, and Akron. In December, she danced in and out of twenty-one cities, including Charleston, Dayton, Omaha, Nashville, Des Moines, and Chicago. The company continued on tour through January 1915 and then took a February break. The hectic touring schedule began again in March and carried through July.

During this tour, Anna introduced two new solo works. She had created these herself, and they reflected her passion for nature. In New York, she premiered *Dragonfly,* a dance that mimicked the swift, darting movements of the insect. Anna designed the shimmering purple, green, and blue costume herself. In San Francisco, she debuted *Californian Poppy.* In this solo, the unique costume she had designed allowed her to close the petals of the flower over her, imitating a poppy as it closes up when evening falls. The audience was delighted with this tribute to their local flower, and both *Californian Poppy* and *Dragonfly* became popular favorites.

While her dancers took time off in August 1915, Anna didn't stop to rest. She went to Chicago and California to be filmed in the starring role of Fenella for *The Dumb Girl of Portici,* a film for Universal Studios. Most of the film required acting, not dancing. It didn't take long, however, for Anna to learn to apply her genius for expressing emotion to the screen-acting style of the day.

Although Anna's role came out well, the film was not a box office success. Anna felt that films did not capture the true spirit of dance. But she did enjoy the people she met in Hollywood.

In 1916, Anna accepted an engagement at the Hippodrome in New York City. The Hippodrome was a huge theater that seated more than five thousand people. Anna and her troupe were part of "The Big Show," which included hundreds of performers. There were trained elephants and lions and a Mammoth Minstrel Show. Despite being on the bill with variety acts, Anna maintained her high artistic standards. Her company first performed *The Sleeping Beauty* and later presented smaller works such as *Dragonfly, Gavotte,* and *Christmas.* By the end of her five-month appearance, one million people had seen the great Pavlova dance in the Hippodrome.

Because Europe was still engulfed in war in 1917,

crossing the Atlantic would be risky. Anna made the decision to tour Latin America instead. Her company traveled throughout Central and South America. All along the way, they gave concerts to benefit the Red Cross and help the war effort. The dancers sometimes had to endure performances in sweltering heat and humidity. Travel was often uncomfortable—they rode for days on a cattle boat, sleeping one deck above the noise and smell of the animals. Anna showed her concern for the well-being of her dancers, and she made a point of saying a few cheerful words to everyone, even in the most difficult circumstances. The dancers loved and respected her for it. This was the same Madame of whom they were in awe—who moved them to tears as they watched her dance Giselle from the wings, who spoke harshly to them when they did not practice, and who always made sure that wherever they were they had a proper Christmas celebration.

In November 1918, the Great War ended. It was safe to return to England. But Anna still had months of commitments to fulfill in South America.

She was always interested in learning the folk dances of the places she visited, and she tried to find the best local teachers to instruct her company. Then she would adapt the dances to her style of dancing.

In Mexico City, she performed *Mexican Dances.* Her final concerts there were performed in the open air on a stage built in the bullring. She wanted people who were too poor to go to the ballet to be able to see her. When Anna danced a sort of Mexican hat dance on her toes around a sombrero, the audience went wild with appreciation, tossing their own sombreros onstage.

In Buenos Aires, Anna debuted a new dance that she had been thinking about for a long time. She called it *Autumn Leaves.* In this dance, Anna was the last chrysanthemum of autumn. Caught up by a cold wind, she was tossed about with the falling leaves, then rescued by a poet who loved her. Finally, she was abandoned to the north wind again. Of all her dances, this one was closest to her heart, and Anna was most particular about how the company performed *Autumn Leaves.* It usually took many, many rehearsals to meet her standards.

By the autumn of 1919, Anna had fulfilled her engagements in South America. On November 4, 1919, she finally set sail for Europe. At last, after five years, she was going home to Ivy House.

6

Legend

The curtain was about to rise on a performance of *Snowflakes.* In a playful mood, wearing her lovely tutu, Anna unexpectedly began to do a hilarious imitation of her friend Charlie Chaplin as the Little Tramp. There was Anna, swinging an imaginary cane and tipping an imaginary bowler hat, hamming it up. With the curtain rising, it was all the dancers could do to begin the ballet and keep from laughing. Anna stood watching from the wings with a mischievous grin.

Even though she did not have children of her own, Anna loved children. After the Great War, she established a home in Paris for orphaned Russian girls.

The charity performances she gave did not always cover expenses for the orphanage, so she used her own money to support the home. It delighted Anna to visit the girls. She saw to it that each one was trained in a profession and that the home provided an atmosphere of beauty and simplicity.

Wherever she went, Anna used her exceptional gifts to open new eyes to the beauty of classical dance. She remained committed to what she saw as her mission to bring ballet to the world. Her tours not only took her back to America and throughout Europe time and again, but also to Australia, New Zealand, and South Africa. She traveled the East—stages in Japan, China, the Philippines, Burma, India, and Egypt were graced with her talent. Her fame and reputation remained unsurpassed. Her pace never slackened.

Anna felt it was her duty to encourage young dancers. She showed special regard for the children who came backstage to meet "the legendary Pavlova." She always left them with the memory of a warm hug and words of encouragement from Madame.

After a performance in Los Angeles, a little girl dressed in a blue silk dress was introduced to Anna as a promising ballet student. Anna congratulated the awestruck child and gave her a few pink carnations and cherry blossoms from one of her own bouquets.

With a graceful flourish, Anna bent down and kissed the little dancer, who could only wordlessly clutch the flowers and gaze at Madame through a mist of tears.

In December 1930, when she was almost fifty, Anna finished a tour of England and went to Cannes, France, to rest over the holidays. On her way to Paris from Cannes, the train she was riding was involved in an accident. Anna went outside in the cold to see if she could help.

In Paris, she had a cough and fever but, as always, rehearsed anyway. Against her doctor's advice, she boarded a train for The Hague, Netherlands, where her next tour was to start. When she arrived, she went straight to bed because she was having difficulty breathing. Anna's condition worsened, though her doctors did what they could. She died in the early hours of Friday, January 23, 1931, after whispering to Victor to prepare the swan costume.

Anna had insisted to Victor that her dancers perform a charity concert in Brussels on Sunday, without her if need be. At the conclusion of the concert, as cello and harp played "The Swan," a spotlight swept the empty stage. The audience stood, remembering the beauty of what had been.

Afterword

By its nature, the art of dance is fleeting, existing only for the moment. All that remains of Anna Pavlova's genius are the glowing yet somehow inadequate descriptions of how she moved and of how people were moved by her. Photographs reveal hints of her exceptional grace and delicate charm. Though Anna made attempts to have her dancing recorded, the films of her day could not satisfactorily capture her artistry. But the spirit of Anna Pavlova lives on in the tradition of dance. She did much to win popular support for her art. The prima ballerina who was trained in an exclusive ballet system intended for the Russian elite brought her art to people the world over.

Everywhere she went, Anna inspired and encouraged the young. Thousands of children who saw her dance were inspired to dance themselves. The little girl in the blue silk dress, one of hundreds to whom Anna gave flowers over the years, grew up to become one of America's most beloved choreographers. Agnes de Mille treasured her flowers for years. She credited Anna with changing her life.

Anna Pavlova was more than a gifted technician and a genius of expression. Never was her sole purpose to gather fame and fortune for herself. She had a selfless devotion to the art of dance. Her driving ambition was to lead audiences to discover the soaring beauty that could carry their spirits upward. Anna believed that in expressing beauty, humankind advances a step forward. She was the world's ambassador of the beauty that is dance.

Selected Repertoire

Here are a few of the roles Anna Pavlova danced in her lifetime.
Entries are given by the date of Anna's first performance.

	BALLET	ROLE	COMPOSER	CHOREOGRAPHER
1898	*The Two Stars*	Star	Pugni	Petipa
	Daughter of the Pharaoh	Pas de trois	Pugni	Petipa
1899	*The Imaginary Dryads*	Daughter of the Count	Pugni	Gerdt
1900	*The Seasons*	Hoarfrost	Glazunov	Petipa
	The Awakening of Flora	Flora	Drigo	Petipa, Ivanov
1901	*The Nutcracker*	Golden Waltz	Tchaikovsky	Ivanov
1902	*La Bayadère*	Nikiya	Minkus	Petipa
1903	*Daughter of the Pharaoh*	Ramsea	Pugni	Petipa
	Giselle	Giselle	Adam	Petipa
1905	*Don Quixote*	Kitri	Minkus, Drigo	Petipa, Gorsky
1907	*Chopiniana*	Pas de deux	Chopin	Fokine
	The Dying Swan	Swan	Saint-Saëns	Fokine
1908	*The Sleeping Beauty*	Aurora	Tchaikovsky	Petipa
	Egyptian Nights	Veronica	Arensky	Fokine
1909	*Swan Lake*	Odette-Odile	Tchaikovsky	Petipa, Ivanov
	Les Sylphides	Sylphide	Chopin	Fokine
	The Nutcracker	Spanish Dancer	Tchaikovsky	Ivanov
1910	*Coppélia*	Swanilda	Delibes	Saint-Léon, Saracco
	Le Papillon	Butterfly	Minkus	Pavlova
	Giselle	Giselle	Adam	Gorsky, Mordkin
1911	*Snowflakes*	Snowflake	Tchaikovsky	Pavlova
	Giselle	Giselle	Adam	Ballet Russes production
1912	*Amarilla*	Amarilla	Glazunov	Zajlich
1913	*Giselle*	Giselle	Adam	Petipa, Pavlova, Clustine
1915	*Dragonfly*	Dragonfly	Kreisler	Pavlova
	Californian Poppy	Poppy	Tchaikovsky	Pavlova
1916	*The Sleeping Beauty*	Aurora	Tchaikovsky	Petipa, Clustine
1919	*Mexican Dances*	Mexican girl	Padilla	traditional
	Autumn Leaves	Chrysanthemum	Chopin	Pavlova
1923	*Japanese Dances*	Japanese girl	Geehl	Fijuma, Fumi
	Krishna and Radha	Radha	Banerji	Shankar

Selected Bibliography

Algeranoff, H. *My Years with Pavlova.* London: William Heineman, 1957.

de Mille, Agnes. *Dance to the Piper.* Boston: Little, Brown, 1951.

Fokine, Michel. "A Choreographer Remembers." In *Pavlova: A Biography*, edited by Arthur Henry Franks. New York: Macmillan, 1956.

Fonteyn, Margot. *Pavlova: Portrait of a Dancer.* New York: Viking, 1984.

Jowitt, Deborah. *Time and the Dancing Image.* Berkeley, CA: University of California Press, 1988.

Kerensky, Oleg. *Anna Pavlova.* New York: E. P. Dutton, 1973.

Kraus, Richard. *History of the Dance in Art and Education.* Englewood Cliffs, NJ: Prentice-Hall, 1969.

Lazzarini, John, and Roberta Lazzarini. *Pavlova: Repertoire of a Legend.* New York: Schirmer Books, 1980.

May, Helen. *The Swan: The Story of Anna Pavlova.* Edinburgh: Thomas Nelson & Sons, 1958.

Migel, Parmenia. *The Ballerinas: From the Court of Louis XIV to Pavlova.* New York: Macmillan, 1972.

Money, Keith. *Pavlova: Her Life and Art.* New York: Alfred A. Knopf, 1982.

Pavlova, Anna. "Pages of My Life." In *Anna Pavlova*, edited by V. Svetloff. New York: Dover Publications, 1974.

——. "Towards a Dream of Art." In *Flight of the Swan: A Memory of Anna Pavlova*, edited by André Olivéroff, as told to John Gill. New York: E. P. Dutton, 1932.

Roslavleva, Natalia. *Era of the Russian Ballet*. New York: E. P. Dutton, 1966.

Smakov, Gennady. *The Great Russian Dancers*. New York: Alfred A. Knopf, 1984.

Société Radio-Canada. *Pavlova*. Directed by Pierre Morin. 81 min. Sony Video, 1983. Videocassette.

Websites

Anna Pavlova - Picture Gallery
<http://www.staff.dmu.ac.uk/~jafowler/pavlova.html>

Creative Quotations from Anna Pavlova
<http://www.bemorecreative.com/one/1291.htm>

Great Ballerinas: Anna Pavlova
<http://www.dancer.com/Pavlova.html>

Index

About the Author

For many years, while **Barbara Allman**'s occupations were teaching and writing, her *preoccupation* was dance. She studied modern dance with Denise Szykula and performed with The Nonce Dance Ensemble, a professional dance troupe, in Detroit. She lives in Jacksonville, Oregon, and works as a freelance writer and editor of educational materials. She is also the author of *Her Piano Sang: A Story about Clara Schumann.*

About the Illustrator

Shelly O. Haas has illustrated sixteen books for children. She enjoys infusing the images in her books with a rich texture of the characters' culture, symbolic identity, and the historic time period that fostered their growth. Shelly and her family live in Harrington, Washington.